Whatever you ask
for in prayer
with faith,
you will receive.

MATTHEW 21:22

PINK Prayer BOOK

Edited by
DIANA LOSCIALE

Liguori

Imprimi Potest
Thomas D. Picton, CSsR
Provincial, Denver Province
The Redemptorists

Copyright © 2008, 2018 Liguori Publications
ISBN 978-0-7648-1767-0

Printed in the United States of America
23 22 21 20 19 / 13 12 11 10 9

Library of Congress Cataloging-in-Publication Data

The pink prayer book / edited by Diana Losciale.
      p. cm.
Includes bibliographical references and index.
   ISBN 978-0-7648-1767-0 (alk. paper)
   1. Cancer—Patients—Prayers and devotions. I. Losciale, Diana.
   BV4910.33.P56 2008
   242'.4—dc22

                                                    2008031977

Scripture quotations are from *New Revised Standard Version Bible,* copyright © 1989 Division of Christian Education of the National Council of the Churches of Christ in the United States of America. Used by permission. All rights reserved.

Excerpt of "Angel's Call" by Bruce A. Edwards, copyright © 2007, used by permission of author.

Prayer by Jeanne Carol Martin is from *Facing Cancer With God's Help: A Personal Journey,* copyright © 2014 Liguori Publications.

Liguori Publications, a nonprofit corporation, is an apostolate of the Redemptorists. To learn more about the Redemptorists, visit Redemptorists.com.

To order, call 800-325-9521.
Liguori.org

Cover design by Wendy Barnes

Contents

Dedication

For all those who shared
their prayers and stories herein,
thank you.

For all those who need words
to pray and cannot find them,
take these.

In memory of Diana Losciale,
who passed away January 16, 2014,
surrounded by her family,
after a brave struggle with cancer.

Introduction

Here in one special book are the prayers, hopes, fears and comforts of women who have had breast cancer and the families affected by the disease. The all-too-common diagnosis of breast cancer can send a woman into such a frightening place that the support of others becomes terribly important—and their prayers essential. This book can turn the "mourning into dancing" for thousands of women.

COKIE ROBERTS
ABC NEWS, NATIONAL PUBLIC RADIO
AUTHOR AND BREAST CANCER SURVIVOR

COPING

Here we sit—you, the doctor, behind that big imposing desk, and me, the impatient patient, restless in my padded chair.

I have so much to do today! I really don't have time to sit here, but the nurse said you prefer to discuss biopsy results in person.

So here we sit. I must quiet my mind, pay attention. If I pay attention, this meeting will be shorter. Besides, I'm sure everything is fine, just fine...

What?

Your voice sounds so far away—what are you saying?

I have cancer? You are telling me I have cancer? I don't understand. Cancer!

No, no—it wasn't supposed to be cancer. Just a cyst, an innocuous lump...Besides, I feel fine. So this can't be true. It's not cancer.

Cancer?

Will I die? Women do die of breast cancer...

Your voice sounds so far away—what are you saying?

All these statistics you recite—what do they have to do with me? How do I know what these numbers mean? How can numbers tell you anything about my situation?

Your muted words float through space, meaningless words that seem to have nothing to do with me.

Yet I am compelled to listen.

Schedule more tests? I am very busy just now, with many obligations and responsibilities. I don't have the time…

You say we will have to wait for test results to determine treatment?

Wait? I don't want to wait!

I need to know now. I need to know right now, this minute, what this means for me, for my family. I need to know what this means, what to expect.

You say I may need surgery?

You say I may need chemotherapy?

You say I may need radiation?

Your voice sounds so far away—what are you saying?

Can you please repeat what you said about treatments?

This is too much information. I can't think about all this. I can't imagine how I could make time for all that. I am very busy just now, with obligations…and responsibilities.

Let's begin again.

You say I have breast cancer? You say this cancer is in my body, attacking my cells, trying to steal my life?

You sound so far away…

"Doctor, are you sure?"

PATRICIA CORRIGAN
SURVIVOR

O Lord,
Are you listening?
I beg your interlude.
I pray for your counsel.
I pray for your guiding hand.
Please take away this fear
    and replace it with hope.
O Holy Mother,
Who will bear this news to our own mother?
O Jesus,
Lead us out of this desert!
Teach us grace.
Hold us; hold us up
as we gather our strength.
Here is my trust in your divine wisdom
Here is my belief in the joy of you.
Please accept my prayer
Please accept my faith,
Please help my sister heal.
I cannot imagine life without her.
I cannot imagine Life without You.

JEAN A. TAYLOR
SISTER

Out of the depths I cry to you, O Lord.
    Lord, hear my voice!
Let your ears be attentive
to the voice of my supplications!

If you, O Lord, should mark iniquities,
    Lord, who could stand?
But there is forgiveness with you,
    so that you may be revered.

I wait for the Lord, my soul waits,
    and in his word I hope;
my soul waits for the Lord
    more than those who watch for the morning,
    more than those who watch for the morning.

O Israel, hope in the Lord!
    For with the Lord there is steadfast love,
    and with him is great power to redeem.
It is he who will redeem Israel
        from all its iniquities.
PSALM 130

I know to hope for the best
and to expect the worst.

Can we know too much?
Is knowledge strength?

I pray for your wisdom
and for serenity.
I pray to be able to handle
whatever the future holds.

KATHY LASS
SURVIVOR

*Whatever you ask for in prayer with faith,
you will receive.*

MATTHEW 21:22

God bless our husbands
And their strong voices.

SHEILA M. CHIBNALL-TREPTOW
SURVIVOR

It is such joy to think that for each pain cheerfully borne we shall love God more through eternity.

THÉRÈSE OF LISIEUX

Therefore, since we are justified by faith, we have peace with God through our Lord Jesus Christ, through whom we have obtained access to this grace in which we stand; and we boast in our hope of sharing the glory of God. And not only that, but we also boast in our sufferings, knowing that suffering produces endurance, and endurance produces character, and character produces hope, and hope does not disappoint us, because God's love has been poured into our hearts through the Holy Spirit that has been given to us.

ROMANS 5:1–5

God,
Please give me the strength to fight
and the strength to heal.
Please keep watch over my children;
allow them the courage
to endure the stages of my healing.
Thank you
For your loving support and
for the encouragement from those around me.
And guard my sense of humor
so I can maintain balance.
Amen.

KATHERINE WELSH
SURVIVOR

Guide me, O Thou great Jehovah,
Pilgrim through this barren land.
I am weak, but Thou art mighty;
Hold me with Thy powerful hand.
Bread of Heaven, Bread of Heaven,
Feed me till I want no more;
Feed me till I want no more.

Open now the crystal fountain,
Whence the healing stream doth flow;
Let the fire and cloudy pillar
Lead me all my journey through.
Strong Deliverer, strong Deliverer,
Be Thou still my Strength and Shield;
Be Thou still my Strength and Shield.

Lord, I trust Thy mighty power,
Wondrous are Thy works of old;
Thou deliver'st Thine from thralldom,
Who for naught themselves had sold:
Thou didst conquer, Thou didst conquer,
Sin, and Satan and the grave,
Sin, and Satan and the grave.

FROM A WELSH HYMN BY WILLIAM WILLIAMS

I feel like Mary Magdalene at your tomb,
But it's me.
I am at the tomb of my cancer-free life,
A phase that has come to its own sudden end.
Can this loss become holy, meaningful?
Can my tears be temporary, like Mary's?
She knew of resurrection but could not imagine
what you meant.
I, too, am fearful.
I, too, am heartbroken.
But you are alive!
And with us always.
Help me to trust today
That the best is yet to come.
Help me
to recognize your voice speaking my name.
Embrace me.
Be with me in the newness of my fear.

SHEILA M. CHIBNALL-TREPTOW
SURVIVOR

My God (oh, let me call thee mine,
Weak, wretched sinner though I be),
My trembling soul would fain be thine;
My feeble faith still clings to thee.

Not only for the past I grieve,
The future fills me with dismay;
Unless Thou hasten to relieve,
Thy suppliant is a castaway.

I cannot say my faith is strong,
I dare not hope my love is great;
But strength and love to thee belong;
Oh, do not leave me desolate!

I know I owe my all to thee;
Oh, take the heart I cannot give!
Do Thou my strength—my Saviour be,
And make me to thy glory live.

ANNE BRONTË

O Lord,
I turn to you for comfort,
For blessing, for strength.
You are my spiritual rock.

I will need to trust others
With my body and my life.
I rely on you, Lord, to guide them.

I fear the tests, the treatments
in my future.
How can I stand it?
Only with your help, Lord.
I know that you will send
People to support me.

You, Lord can help my family
to not be afraid.
Be their rock, too, O Lord.

Help me to adjust.
Help me to find joy and peace.

Let me find the grace to accept your will.
Lord, stay my rock, be my companion.
And help me to be confident
in your continuous love.

SUSAN E. CUDDIHEE
AUNT, COUSIN, DAUGHTER-IN-LAW, FRIEND

God is our refuge and strength,
a very present help in trouble.
Therefore we will not fear, though the earth
should change,
though the mountains shake in the heart
of the sea;
though its waters roar and foam,
though the mountains tremble with its tumult.
Selah

PSALM 46:1-3

Dear Lord,
A second diagnosis...
Are you telling me I have more to learn?
What is your message to me, Lord?
That I have strength?
    That I have control?
    I do.

My blessings are endless,
and for that I always thank you.
Amen.

    MARY JO BLACKWOOD, RN, MPH
    SURVIVOR, SISTER

O shepherd of souls,
O first of Words,
Through which we all were created,
may it please you, may it please:
free us from our fear
and fragility.

    HILDEGARD OF BINGEN

Dear God,
How can this be?
I'm healthy. I have no pain.
There is no such history in my family.
Cancer? How can this be?
Lumpectomy, chemotherapy, radiation—
these words scare me, Lord.
Within minutes
My world has turned upside down.
Will I be OK?
I am afraid, Lord.
I do not know how to tell my family,
my friends.
Father, please guide me through this.

Help me.
Help me help myself and use this
To help others.
Is that what you want?

Please show me the way.
We can do this (whatever this is).
You may have to carry me.

I know there is sunshine behind this cloud.
I know you are there.

I know there is a reason.
I know I will be well again
    because you are with me.
I will pray again tomorrow
    and the next day
    and the next…and for everyone.

DOROTHY CARACCIOLO
SURVIVOR

Dear Lord,
As tears fall, I confess I am afraid.
It is fear of the unknown.
My life spins out of control, and
I do not know where to anchor.

I pray for peace.
You have peace that passes understanding.

I pray for the faith to win this battle.
Please grant me the strength
and courage for this journey
and walk with me, I pray.
Amen.

EVELYN STAFFORD DANIELS
SURVIVOR

You know well what is happening,
my dear Jesus.
I have only you.
Come to my aid.

JEANNE JUGAN

*Cast all your anxiety on him, because he cares
for you. Discipline yourselves; keep alert. Like
a roaring lion your adversary the devil prowls
around, looking for someone to devour. Resist
him, steadfast in your faith, for you know that
your brothers and sisters throughout the world are
undergoing the same kinds of suffering. And after
you have suffered for a little while, the God of all
grace, who has called you to his eternal glory in
Christ, will himself restore, support, strengthen,
and establish you. To him be the power for ever
and ever. Amen.*

1 PETER 5:7–11

O Holy Spirit, I am so in need of your gifts!
There are so many things to consider,
decisions to make, options and protocols
to choose from. What team of doctors shall
I choose? Can I choose treatment? Can I
endure reconstruction? Can I endure no
reconstruction? Please fill me with your gifts
of wisdom and understanding, knowledge and
good counsel, courage, reverence, and piety,
and finally peace with the choices I will make.

SHEILA M. CHIBNALL-TREPTOW
SURVIVOR

Likewise the Spirit helps us in our weakness;
for we do not know how to pray as we ought,
but that very Spirit intercedes with sighs too deep
for words. And God, who searches the heart,
knows what is the mind of the Spirit, because the
Spirit intercedes for the saints according to the
will of God.

ROMANS 8:26–27

HEALING

Here we sit—you, a stranger, on the other side of the tray table, and me, the impatient patient, reclining in my overstuffed chair.

I have very little to do today. My only obligation is to relax here in the chemotherapy lounge, waiting as these potent drugs drip into my body.

Here we sit. You must have cancer too.

How did this happen to us? One minute we were busy, living our lives, dashing from one place to the next, seeing important people, going important places, doing important things.

Then we learned we had cancer.

Cancer!

Other people have cancer. Not me. I feel fine, I told my doctor. There must be some mistake, I said.

There was no mistake.

That seems so long ago—yet only a few weeks have passed. Sometimes I feel as if I've stumbled into a new country; a country with a landscape, a language, and a culture all unfamiliar to me. Though I am a newcomer, I am expected to find my way around, understand everything that is said to me, behave appropriately at all times.

Life in this new country also requires making many decisions, decisions that may well alter the course of my life. I have read the materials, talked with my doctors, and made the decisions.

As I sit here in the chemotherapy lounge next to a stranger, I review those decisions.

The names of the drugs that fight cancer skitter through my mind, chased by lists of potential side effects, all followed by a rundown of options—pharmaceutical and otherwise—for fending off those side effects.

What if I made poor choices?

What if the treatments don't work?

Stop! I tell my mind to stop racing, stop repeating facts, stop reviewing statistics, stop reminding me every minute of every day that I have cancer.

Sometimes I am able to forget. When I first wake in the morning, when I become absorbed in a project, when I slide into a tub filled with warm water after a long day, I am able to forget.

Then the word roars back into my consciousness: *CANCER*.

Hot tears well up, heart pounds, fear returns. I calm myself. I'll be fine, I tell myself. I'll be fine. This is my life now, but this is all temporary. Eventually the treatments will end, and I will be fine.

On my medical chart, I am a cancer patient. In my life, I am so much more. I am a woman with a brain, a strong will, a loving family, and dear friends. I know my way around a garden, an art museum, a forest, a symphony hall, a library, and a farmers' market. I have seen a bit of the world. I have every intention of seeing more.

And I know how to laugh. Remembering how funny I looked in some of the wigs I tried on, I giggle aloud. Sitting there on the other side of the tray table, you look up and smile. I return that smile and introduce myself.

"Hello…"

PATRICIA CORRIGAN
SURVIVOR

No reason to worry, I keep telling myself. Cancer is something that happens to other people. But within twenty-four hours of a simple biopsy, my life lies shattered before me as I struggle with the positive results. With every fiber of my being, I am fearful, desperate. I try to remember everything I have ever heard about chemotherapy and radiation, and I question whether I am strong enough to keep fighting. To keep fighting when my hair falls out. To keep fighting when I am nauseated from the drugs. In my heart, O God, I know I can do this only with your help, that cancer will be just a steppingstone along my journey's path and not a boulder blocking my way. That with the help of family, friends, and faith, I will continue to put my trust in God's plan and take one day at a time.

Hear my plea, O God, I pray.
Guide my steps along the way.

My faith in you will calm my fear
Yours is the voice I long to hear.

Lift the darkness and shine your light
Give me strength to finish the fight.

THERESE SWARTS IVERSON
SURVIVOR

Sing praise for renewal,
and for every mountain we climb.
Sing praise for strength as we heal.
Sing praise for mornings and evenings
and in-between moments.
Sing praise for faith that sustains us always.
Sing praise for sisters and mothers,
for daughters, and friends,
for men and for music and holding of hands.
Sing praises to God; let us all learn to sing,
Ever striving and smiling
as we go through our treatments,
Ever living your message of hope and awe.
Amen.

DIANA LOSCIALE
NIECE

O Blessed Mother,
Mother of Jesus,
You saw your only son be tortured
and die on the cross.
I pray for strength like yours.
I, too, am a simple mother who asks
for your guidance during this
so very difficult time in my life.

Please, Mary, help me. Help me.
I am God's servant, but I am a mother, too.
You know how I feel.

Please help me to be a good mother,
not unlike you.
I do not have the energy
     to speak my thoughts aloud;
please read them.

I pray for God's wishes but
  I need you to pray for me too.
Help me to be kind, thoughtful, loving,
and unselfish.
You and our Lord are so good to me.

Thank you, Mary.
I can sense your presence in my darkest hours.
Thank you for being with me.

ELIZABETH ST. CIN
SURVIVOR

Our Lord has no need of books or teachers to
instruct our souls. He, the Teacher of Teachers,
instructs us without any noise of words.

THÉRÈSE OF LISIEUX

Teach us, good Lord,
to serve thee as thou deservest;
To give and not to count the cost;
To fight and not to heed the wounds;
To toil and not to seek for rest;
To labor and not to ask for any reward
Save that of knowing that we do thy will,
Through Jesus Christ our Lord. Amen.

IGNATIUS LOYOLA

I bless the LORD who gives me counsel;
in the night also my heart instructs me.
Therefore my heart is glad, and my soul rejoices;
my body also rests secure.
You show me the path of life.
In your presence there is fullness of joy;
in your right hand are pleasures for evermore.

PSALM 16:7, 9, 11

Dear Lord,
Please help me remember
that healing is a process,
    that healing takes time.
I am impatient; I want to do so much.
Help me remember the trauma of treatments
    and understand the need to mend.
Help me follow advice I would give to others,
    to take care of myself,
    to pamper myself,
    to love myself, and
    to give my body time
    to heal.
Amen.

KATHERINE WELSH
SURVIVOR

I give thanks for the faith that drives me
I look to my higher power to help me
understand what I've lost and what I've gained
And to keep hope in my heart.

MIRNA RAFAEL-REYES
MARSHA LYNNE FLOWERS
SURVIVORS

You are truly the God of the light
and of the dark.
From each of the low places
to which I've been dropped,
You have lifted me up with great blessing.
The love, kindness, and thoughtfulness
that surrounds me
is the amazingly tangible experience of you.

SHEILA M. CHIBNALL-TREPTOW
SURVIVOR

Rise up, my soul, rise up, shake off the dust, lift
yourself up, and enter before the gaze of the Lord,
your God, to confess before him all the mercy
and compassion that he has shown to you.

Blessed are you, Adonai,
in the firmament of heaven.
Let all the marrow and virtue of my spirit
bless you.
Let all the substance of my soul and body
bless you.
Let all that is within me glorify you.

GERTRUDE THE GREAT OF HELFTA

My Sweet Lord:
If this is as bad as it gets, I can handle it.
So many endure so much more.
I have means.
I have my sisters, my husband, my son.
I feel good.
Why do I have it so easy?
I pray for those who are younger, juggling
exhaustion, treatment, and small children with
difficult questions, crying for reassurance.

What dues am I to pay for this, Lord?
What should I do to be fully grateful
     for this fortune?
To help other women struggling with this?
Your guidance? Please.
Amen.

MARY JO BLACKWOOD, RN, MPH
SURVIVOR, SISTER

O LORD, you have searched me and known me.
You know when I sit down and when I rise up;
you discern my thoughts from far away.
You search out my path and my lying down,
and are acquainted with all my ways.
Even before a word is on my tongue,
O LORD, you know it completely.
You hem me in, behind and before,
and lay your hand upon me.
Such knowledge is too wonderful for me;
it is so high that I cannot attain it.

Where can I go from your spirit?
Or where can I flee from your presence?
If I ascend to heaven, you are there;
if I make my bed in Sheol, you are there.
If I take the wings of the morning
and settle at the farthest limits of the sea,
even there your hand shall lead me,
and your right hand shall hold me fast.

If I say, "Surely the darkness shall cover me,
and the light around me become night",
even the darkness is not dark to you;
the night is as bright as the day,
for darkness is as light to you.

For it was you who formed my inward parts;
you knit me together in my mother's womb.
I praise you, for I am fearfully and
    wonderfully made.
Wonderful are your works; that I know very well.
My frame was not hidden from you,
when I was being made in secret,
intricately woven in the depths of the earth.
Your eyes beheld my unformed substance.
In your book were written
all the days that were formed for me,
when none of them as yet existed.
How weighty to me are your thoughts, O God!
How vast is the sum of them!
I try to count them—they are more than the sand;
I come to the end—I am still with you.

O that you would kill the wicked, O God,
and that the bloodthirsty would depart from me—
those who speak of you maliciously,
and lift themselves up against you for evil!
Do I not hate those who hate you, O Lord?
And do I not loathe those who rise up against you?
I hate them with perfect hatred;
I count them my enemies.
Search me, O God, and know my heart;
test me and know my thoughts.
See if there is any wicked way in me,
and lead me in the way everlasting.

PSALM 139

Are not two sparrows sold for a penny? Yet not
one of them will fall to the ground unperceived by
your Father. And even the hairs of your head are
all counted. So do not be afraid; you are of more
value than many sparrows.

MATTHEW 10:29–31

O God,
Since you had counted every hair on my head
(and there were a lot),
Count now my bald head as precious
as was my newborn child's.

SHEILA M. CHIBNALL-TREPTOW
SURVIVOR

*"Do not let your hearts be troubled. Believe in
God, believe also in me. In my Father's house
there are many dwelling-places. If it were not so,
would I have told you that I go to prepare a place
for you? And if I go and prepare a place for you,
I will come again and will take you to myself, so
that where I am, there you may be also. And you
know the way to the place where I am going."*

JOHN 14:1–4

*If in my name you ask me for anything,
I will do it.*

JOHN 14:14

O Heavenly Father,
I humbly beseech blessings for my family.
Keep my loved ones in
    your tender care and protect them
    from every evil.
Grant that no matter how separated we may be
by distance,
We shall always be close to one another and
    to you in the sacred heart of your son,
Jesus.
May we continue to grow in love and peace,
ever seeking your blessings
    until we are united with you forever in
heaven.
Amen.

ELIZABETH ST. CIN
SURVIVOR

*For I will restore health to you,
and your wounds I will heal, says the LORD.*
JEREMIAH 30:17

O God,
From the moment of the diagnosis,
Nothing else mattered.
I could not hear.

I prayed daily.
I prayed to relax.
I listened to the sound of ocean waves
and thunderstorms.
I imagined those storms
fighting the battle within.
And I was calmed.

O God, I want to be healthy,
As healthy as the sea filled with all the life
within it.

And with that thought, with that petition,
Suddenly, I knew:
I knew you would help me survive.

NANCY DONALDSON
SURVIVOR

SURVIVING

Here we sit—you, the doctor, on the low stool in the examining room, and me, the impatient patient, squirming on the table.

I have so much to do. Who wouldn't, on the last day of radiation treatments? This is an important day for me, and I am eager to get into my clothing and out of the building.

So here we sit. I must quiet my mind, pay attention. If I pay attention, this meeting will be shorter. Not that I find this to be a particularly difficult conversation...

What?

Your voice sounds calm and confident as you tell me that as of now, everything looks good. As of now, I am a cancer survivor, ready to begin to distance myself from the diagnosis and treatment, from this difficult period. Yes, I understand that my health will be carefully monitored for years to come.

What are you saying?

I see. Apparently, some people do not look forward to the last day of treatment. Instead, some people fear that day, because they think they have stopped fighting and the enemy may attack once again.

What do I think?

I think I am ready to reclaim my life, to get back to normal. Yes, I know nothing will ever be quite the same again, but I am ready to embrace the new normal, whatever that turns out to be. With the help of all my doctors, I have made good treatment decisions. My medical team has provided excellent care and plenty of emotional support. But what a relief it will be to see fewer medical appointments on the calendar and have more time to spend with my family and friends!

Still, I would be lying if I said I will never think about the possibility of recurrence. Over these past months, I have frequently wrestled with fear, fear that springs from not knowing how long I will live, whether I will have to go through this again.

But I am determined not to live under that black cloud. I am prepared to walk out of this office, into the sunshine, into my future.

Right now, right here, on this momentous day, I am deciding I will not live the rest of my life in fear. Instead, in the spirit of moving on, I will respect cancer rather than fear it. For that reason, I will keep all my follow-up appointments, participate in all the monitoring you deem necessary.

You say I have learned one of the most important lessons cancer teaches?

So many survivors speak of those lessons, lessons that changed how they live. I cannot say I fully understand that yet.

I do know I must pace myself these next few months, give my body time to heal. I realize now how important it is to listen to my body. I never understood that before. Now, every day, even when I'm busy, I will make time to notice how I feel, to determine what my body needs, whether that is rest, protein, or a hug from a child.

One more thing: Every day, I will take time to be grateful I am here. I may not have a lot of stamina, I may not have a full head of hair—but I am grateful for this second chance to craft a life.

"Good-bye, Doctor. Thank you."

PATRICIA CORRIGAN
SURVIVOR

Lord,
I feel like the desperate father
of the demon-possessed boy in the Gospel
of Mark.
As he did,
I cry out in the midst of my fear and distress:
"I believe! Help my unbelief!"

Lord, I do believe. Help my unbelief!
Lord, I trust in you. Help my lack of trust!
Lord, I hope in your promises. Fill me when
my hope is failing!

KAY SULLIVAN
FRIEND

"Now sing!" said Life, reissuing to the stars;
And wrung a new note from my wounded side.

So came we to clear spaces, and the sea.
And now I felt its volume in my heart,
And my heart waxed with it,
and Life played on me
The song of the Infinite.
"Now the stars," she said.

EDITH WHARTON

Dear God,
Please put me where you want me to be...
And give me the strength to be there.

> SUSAN THOMPSON
> SURVIVOR

I would like the Angels of Heaven
to be amongst us.
I would like the abundance of peace.
I would like the full vessels of charity.
I would like rich treasures of mercy.
I would like cheerfulness to preside over all.
I would like the friends of Heaven
    to be gathered around
us from all parts.
I would like myself to be a rent-payer
to the Lord; that I
should suffer distress and that He would
bestow a good
blessing upon me.

> BRIGID OF IRELAND

Thank you, God, for my sister.
I will travel with her through
    Whatever her cancer costs her,
    whether it is
    fear or pain or humility or time,
    to reach healing.
I will not falter.
Thank you for the
    special strength siblings share.
Thank you for turbans.
Thank you for summer afternoons
    and clear winter nights.
Thank you for big comfy couches
    where we loll and reminisce,
    holding hands across the memories.
Thank you for the healing, for the brilliant
moments of looking ahead.
Thank you for our spouses who are thoughtful
    and understand our time together.
Thank you for her smile.
Thank you for her valor.
Thank you for healing.
Thank you for tomorrow.

Thank you, God, for hearing our joyful noise.
We are stronger forever in your holy name.
Amen.

JEAN A. TAYLOR
SISTER

I lift up my eyes to the hills—
from where will my help come?
My help comes from the LORD,
who made heaven and earth.
He will not let your foot be moved;
he who keeps you will not slumber.
He who keeps Israel
will neither slumber nor sleep.
The LORD is your keeper;
the LORD is your shade at your right hand.
The sun shall not strike you by day,
nor the moon by night.
The LORD will keep you from all evil;
he will keep your life. The LORD will keep
your going out and your coming in
from this time on and for evermore.

PSALM 121

My daily prayer is...

...for the world to believe that breast cancer wellness is truly possible.

...for wellness to begin this very moment.

...for everyone diagnosed with breast cancer to become uplifted.

...for everyone to be empowered by the experience.

My prayer and invitation is...

...for each of us to experience healing and wellness
   to the fullest.

BEVERLY VOTE
SURVIVOR

Beloved, I pray that all may go well with you and that you may be in good health, just as it is well with your soul.

3 JOHN 1:2

Today rough storms are headed my way.
I will not hide, nor do it alone.
To think of the possibility of death,
what's important?

The Lord is my strength, he will give me courage.

Making huge decisions in a matter of seconds.
Building breasts from my tummy,
no secrets here.
An open door, let go of the things that aren't,
I have the power.

I came with nothing, I will leave with nothing!

Chemo is temporary, no denial here.
The crashing waves come with no warning.
I have lost the wind in my sail,
I am not in control.

*I knew it would pass, minute by minute,
day by day.*

My support parade marches in,
deep concern worn on their sleeves.
Flowers, pink ribbons, and warm ginger tea;
it's important to cry.
To learn how difficult it was in taking the gift.

There are rewards for accepting the help
people want to give.

Food arriving like manna from heaven,
the blessings I have received.
Spending time with my daughter,
so generously given.
She holds my head and says I love you,
Mommy.

Her closeness has turned darkness to light.

The scars are fading and more meaningless.
Feelings are returning.
My hair, how cute; would not have done it
any other way.

I have been inspired, I will not hide.

My mother was taken by this terrible disease.
My life turned upside down.
All the things she taught us, like the wind
beneath my wings.

Steer the ship of my life, heavenly Father.

Let me feel the flow of your grace
as I feel my wounds.
New breasts brought wisdom, strength,
and even more courage.
On a new journey I am about to embark,
determined to live, to give, and to love.

How I have learned, how well I listen.

Sharing myself for others to hear,
I have been inspired.
I make a difference in this world today.
Living in a Sea of Pink, with desires to help
others survive.

Lord, give me the understanding to know why.

CHEF MARY STODOLA
SURVIVOR

Lord,
For sparing my life to see this beautiful day,
for giving me strength to walk this journey, and
for providing family and friends to lend
support and love,
I thank you.

For doctors whose hands and hearts you guide,
for the wisdom you give them to do
what's best for me,
for the nurses and all others who rally round
about me in my struggle,
I thank you.

For the beauty I see when I look in the mirror,
looking deeply, past the bald head and marbled,
scarred chest,
I thank you.

Thank you for bringing me safely
to this point along the way
where I can begin to see the light
in the distance and
know I am going to make it
with your help.

Gratitude for these blessings fill my heart today,
and I want to say
thank you.
Amen.

EVELYN STAFFORD DANIELS
SURVIVOR

Do not fear, for I am with you,
do not be afraid, for I am your God;
I will strengthen you, I will help you,
I will uphold you with my victorious right hand.

ISAIAH 41:10

For surely I know the plans I have for you,
says the LORD, plans for your welfare and
not for harm, to give you a future with hope.

JEREMIAH 29:11

Center your heart,
Cultivate your spirit!

MIDGE BREMER
SURVIVOR

My Dear Lord:
Doing nothing is
	the most difficult part of this battle.
First surgery; then follow-ups.
I was busy, doing something—fighting.
Now that's over.

What's next?
I'm back to life.
Yet it is not the life I left.
Things have changed.

I'm orderly.
I need to know where to file "this."
Am I cured this time?
I will not go through life
	waiting for the other shoe to drop.

Help me find a way, Lord,
Help me find a balance of
	caution, optimism, and full-throttle living!
I need your guidance.
Amen.

MARY JO BLACKWOOD, RN, MPH
SURVIVOR, SISTER

The times we shared
Were always fun
You made me laugh
And never run
Taught me how
To stand my ground
To pay attention
To every sound
Our lives are short
Yet we'll be remembered
As people who cared
And gave everyone shelter
From their pain and grief
You brought happiness
To a place of misery.

I will catch you
When you fall.

BRUCE A. EDWARDS
NEPHEW

THRIVING

Here we sit—you, my dear friend with the sad eyes, and me, your patient confidante, ready to hear your news now that we have settled into comfortable chairs at the coffee shop.

I have nothing to do today that is more important than spending time with you, listening to you, and learning what is causing you so much distress. You called this morning to ask me to meet with you, and I have been concerned ever since.

So here we sit. You sip your coffee. You take a deep breath. You look at me. What is it? Whatever it is, I'm sure everything will be fine...

What?

Your voice sounds so far away—what are you saying?

You have cancer? You are telling me you have cancer? This can't be true.

Not cancer!

Not cancer...

You recount the story of the biopsy, a biopsy you told no one about. You describe the agonizing wait for the lab report. You revisit the terrifying conversation with the doctor. You have cancer. You have cancer, and you are afraid you will die.

Your voice sounds so far away—what are you saying?

You recite the statistics. You are convinced they have something to do with your situation, that the numbers hold the power to determine your future.

I reach for your hand as your words spill out, cover the table, spread through the room; words that express your fear, your frustration, your emotional pain; words I have heard before, coming from my own crushed spirit.

Yet I am compelled to listen and to remember…

You tell me you must have more tests. You tell me you are very busy just now, with many obligations and responsibilities, that you cannot imagine making time for this. You report you will have to wait once again, this time for results of those tests to determine treatment.

Tears spring to your eyes. I hand you a tissue. You blurt out that you don't want to wait, that you need to know now, right this minute, what this means for you and for your family. You need to know exactly what to expect, what your life will be like as you go through surgery, chemotherapy, and radiation.

Your voice sounds so far away—what are you saying?

Are you saying you are an impatient patient, a cowardly person, a person who cannot imagine coping with cancer treatments?

I encourage you to take another sip of coffee, to take another deep breath. Then I take both your hands in mine. I look into your eyes.

"Listen to me. I know just how you feel. I was an impatient patient. I was a cowardly person. I could not imagine coping with cancer treatments. And yet I did. Here I am today—healthy, happy, and grateful to be alive.

"You will accommodate cancer in your life, but you will not allow cancer to define you. You will cope with each day, pacing yourself as you heal, taking the time your body needs. You will survive to build a new normal for yourself. And then you will thrive, living in gratitude, moving forward in your life, surrounded by those who love you."

PATRICIA CORRIGAN
SURVIVOR

Give her strength to face all the actions
she will bear,
Grant her understanding for all the unknown
she must meet,
Bring her courage in all she must battle.

Bless her with great wisdom,
Help her overcome her fears and doubts,
Let her discover her many great gifts
from within.

Heal her and embrace her
with great confidence,
Bless her with kindness and compassion,
Make her a source of energy for others.

Allow her to face each new day with joy;
offering hope to all,
With arms uplifted,
we pray for this disease to be erased
    so that others may never have to suffer.

Embrace the Army of Earth Angels
dressed in Pink;
    make them whole and restore them to
complete health.

JOANNE POHL
SISTER

Seek peace in your own place. You cannot find
peace anywhere save in your own self.

RABBI BUNAM

O God, thank you for the ancient, heartfelt
prayers
    that run through my head,
    sometimes as a plea,
    sometimes as praise.

SHEILA M. CHIBNALL-TREPTOW
SURVIVOR

The Lord is my light and my salvation;
whom shall I fear?
The Lord is the stronghold of my life;
of whom shall I be afraid?

PSALM 27:1

One time our good Lord said: *All thing shall be well*; and another time he said: *Thou shalt see thyself that all MANNER [of] thing shall be well*.

Dame Julian of Norwich

Precious Jesus,
Thank you for bringing me safely
    through my struggle.
Thank you for every hard day,
    for every tear shed,
    for every difficult trial I passed, and
    for those I failed.
Each bump in the road helped mold me into
the being I have become today.
You have taught me to stand firmly
    for what is right for me.
My trials have brought me to a place where I
can love who I am, and
    for that I am thankful to you.
Tears have turned to sunshine on my face, and
    my heart is filled with love for my sisters
on this journey.

I am so thankful, Lord, that you spared my life
    to help another along the way.
I know I was spared to reach out to some other
frightened soul
    who has just heard the dreadful sentence.
    I thank you for the chance
    to say to her, "You, too, can make it."
My blessings are too numerous to count;
    and I am thankful for them all.
It is with deep love and gratitude
I offer my praise to you, dear Lord.
Amen.

EVELYN STAFFORD DANIELS
SURVIVOR

*For everything there is a season, and a time for
every matter under heaven: a time to be born, and
a time to die; a time to plant, and a time to pluck
up what is planted; a time to kill, and a time to
heal; a time to break down, and a time to build
up; a time to weep, and a time to laugh; a time
to mourn, and a time to dance; a time to throw
away stones, and a time to gather stones together;
a time to embrace, and a time to refrain from
embracing; a time to seek, and a time to lose; a
time to keep, and a time to throw away; a time to
tear, and a time to sew; a time to keep silence, and
a time to speak; a time to love, and a time to hate;
a time for war, and a time for peace.*

ECCLESIASTES 3:1-8

Thank you, God,
for the life that flows through me and
for every bit of my body
that celebrates in the perfection in which
you created it to work.
I resist any worries.

Pain, be gone!
Sickness will not exist in me.

Lord,
Thank you for holding me
during those rough times,
    for hearing my cries.
You helped me stay brave through it all.
My heart will always beat
with the rhythm of life!
You know our souls are full of music.
I will always dance.

I am truly blessed.
I will fulfill my days in health and
    joy with my family and friends.

Sing praises!

MARCI SEABAUGH
SURVIVOR

For nothing will be impossible with God.
LUKE 1:37

Dear Heavenly Father,
Thank you for your faithfulness,
we know you are with us always,
and I pray you will help us
through this crisis in our lives.
You are the Great Physician and
we know you love us with an
everlasting love.
Thank you for healing my daughter,
in Jesus' name, I pray.

ROCHELLE WILLIAMS
MOTHER

*Cast all your anxiety on him,
because he cares for you.*
1 PETER 5:7

Thank you
for another day of beating the odds
with a strong will,
with the perseverance to understand,
a tremendous amount of rejoicing, and
with incredible laughter and love.

RANDEE ELIZABETH KADZIEL
SURVIVOR

For surely I know the plans I have for you,
says the Lord, plans for your welfare and not
for harm, to give you a future with hope.
Then when you call upon me and come and
pray to me, I will hear you.

JEREMIAH 29:11–12

Lord,

The lessons keep coming. You have made me an "expert" for twice surviving. I'm asked to help others. My circle of friends widens. I give them small boxes with prayers of hope tucked inside. I talk to their husbands and families, to help and support them. The women talk to me, expressing what they don't say to their families to protect them, to avoid scaring them, to make them more comfortable.

We talk safely of our deepest thoughts. Is this what you meant for me? I do it gladly. But Lord, please know it is much easier to do with acquaintances. I never thought you would give me my sister's suffering. I thought I had twice paid their price of admission and they, all three, were home free. Yet in your wisdom, you gave me another precious gift. This sister, this stricken one, was the most distanced until this, our shared experience. Thank you for a close bond I would never have predicted. You have lessened her fear by example of my experience.

You have empowered her by my experience to manage her own care.

Your greatest gift to me, dear Lord, has been the tightening of our sisterhood, four sisters bound in sickness and in health and in fierce loyalty. They enrich my life in a special way that makes me want to be the very best I can for the rest of whatever life you grant me. Amen.

MARY JO BLACKWOOD, RN, MPH
SURVIVOR, SISTER

Do not fear, for I am with you, do not be afraid, for I am your God; I will strengthen you, I will help you, I will uphold you with my victorious right hand.

ISAIAH 41:10

Make a joyful noise to the Lord, all the earth.
Worship the Lord with gladness;
come into his presence with singing.
Know that the Lord is God.
It is he that made us, and we are his;
we are his people, and the sheep of his pasture.
Enter his gates with thanksgiving,
and his courts with praise.
Give thanks to him, bless his name.
For the Lord is good;
his steadfast love endures for ever,
and his faithfulness to all generations.

PSALM 100

Anne is stretching her limbs. Her body tuning up for the breast cancer 10K march. She is young, vibrant, a survivor. She can tell you the dark struggles of her days with cancer, but she would rather speak of her hope, her future. Hope is a thing with feathers, and Anne is going to fly in the upcoming march.

PAUL COURY, C.SS.R.
FRIEND

Thank you, Lord,
for giving us this cross to bear.
It is a permanent reminder of how precious
life is and how lucky we are to wake up every
morning to a sun that is shining and the
beauty of the entire world. I see life differently
today than I ever have before. I notice the
birds singing, the deer in the field, the rabbit's
nest, the smell of honeysuckle, and the bright
greens, yellows, reds, and pinks. I never pass a
rose bush without loving its scent and thanking
you for this awesome world we live in. Thanks
for giving my sister this second chance to be
here for our family, friends, and neighbors.
Amen.

HELEN GREAVES
SISTER

I call to you, O God:
Give me what I need to live!
You have good plans for me;
I may see you and know you.

HILDEGARD OF BINGEN

While not considering this disease a blessing,
I must say thank you.
Thank you for giving me such
a beautiful example of strength.
Thank you for showing me
what true courage looks like.
Thank you for blessing our family with the
presence of someone so loving, so strong.
This disease takes lives every year, every
month, every day,
yet my grandmother was spared.
For this, please know my unbound gratitude.

DANIELLE ELLIOTT SMITH
GRANDDAUGHTER

Do not fear to tell Jesus that you love him,
even though you may not feel that love.
In this way you will compel Him to come
to your aid, and to carry you like a little child
who is too weak to walk.

THÉRÈSE OF LISIEUX

My heartfelt thanks to our almighty God and
his healing touch,
Bless me with continued good health.
Enlighten me so I can help others,
Grant me strength to overcome any adversities.
Help me eliminate any undue fears,
Embrace me with your divine wisdom,
Instill me with confidence,
Fill my heart with compassion
as I offer understanding,
Allow me to be joyful each day,
showing hope to all.
Bestow me with the ability
to comfort those in need,
Watch over me and all my sisters.
Thank you for each day,
And the hope for tomorrow
with a healed body and soul.
Amen.

> PATI SLAY
> SURVIVOR

You have turned my mourning into dancing;
you have taken off my sackcloth
and clothed me with joy,
so that my soul may praise you and not be silent.
O Lord my God,
I will give thanks to you for ever.

PSALMS 30:11–12

Give me strength, O Lord, my God!
In times of trouble, I find solace in you.
You are my God,
You are my Creator.

Lord, you have many names,
but I call on God my healer,
the Ultimate Healer.
I humbly deliver a petition of prayer directly
from my heart to yours.
I ask that you heal my heart, touch my body,
anoint my mind, and richly bless my soul.

I realize that all of these entities
have been impacted
by the stressors of everyday life
which, I have resolved, allow me no control.

But you, O Lord, always provide respite.
Now I elevate my faith above my pain,
and my focus and faith are in you, dear Lord.
O God, my healer and my strength!
Help me to not complain but to thank you,
    for you are an awesome God.

I believe you hear and answer prayer.
How do I know?
I am a survivor by divine nature.
Remind me that every day is a blessing,
and in every moment I treasure the time
in which I can relish your presence
forevermore.

This I pray in the mighty name of Jesus,
Amen.

MONICA CASTON
DAUGHTER, COUSIN

Closing Prayer

May the God of life be with you,
calming your fears
and teaching you to trust
in his gracious love and mercy.

May you be strengthened for your fight,
and guided to choices for healing
and wholeness.

And may you be filled with joy and peace
in experiencing God's presence
on your journey.

FROM *FACING CANCER WITH GOD'S HELP:
A PERSONAL JOURNEY*
BY JEANNE CAROL MARTIN

Contributors

Mary Jo Blackwood, RN, MPH
Survivor, sister

Midge Bremer
Survivor

Dorothy Caracciolo
Survivor

Monica Caston
Daughter, cousin

Sheila M. Chibnall-Treptow
Survivor

Patricia Corrigan
Survivor

Paul Coury, CSsR
Friend

Susan E. Cuddihee
Aunt, cousin,
daughter-in-law, friend

Evelyn Stafford Daniels
Survivor

Nancy Donaldson
Survivor

Bruce A. Edwards
Nephew

Marsha Lynne Flowers
Survivor

Helen Greaves
Sister

Therese Swarts Iverson
Survivor

Randee Elizabeth Kadziel
Survivor

Kathy Lass
Survivor

Diana Losciale
Niece

Joanne Pohl
Sister

Mirna Rafael-Reyes
Survivor

Marci Seabaugh
Survivor

Pati Slay
Survivor

Danielle Elliott Smith
Granddaughter

Elizabeth St. Cin
Survivor

Chef Mary Stodola
Survivor

Kay Sullivan
Friend

Jean A. Taylor
Sister

Susan Thompson
Survivor

Beverly Vote
Survivor

Katherine Welsh
Survivor

Rochelle Williams
Mother

Pamela Zell
Daughter

For nothing
will be impossible
with God.

LUKE 1:37